Scones, Muffins & Tea Cakes

Breakfast Breads and Teatime Spreads

Edited with Introduction by Heidi Haughy Cusick

Photography by Deborah Jones and Kathryn Kleinman
Featuring recipes from the Country Garden Cookbook *series:*
Apples *by Christopher Idone* • Berries *by Sharon Kramis* • Corn *by David Tanis*
Greens *by Sibella Kraus* • Herbs *by Rosalind Creasy and Carole Saville*
Lemons *by Christopher Idone* • Onions *by Jesse Ziff Cool* • Pears *by Janet Hazen*
Squash *by Regina Schrambling* • Summer Fruit *by Edon Waycott*
Tomatoes *by Jesse Ziff Cool*

CollinsPublishersSanFrancisco
A Division of HarperCollins*Publishers*

First published in USA 1996 by Collins Publishers San Francisco
Copyright © 1996 Collins Publishers San Francisco
See additional copyright information on page 96.
Series Editor: Meesha Halm
Art Direction: Kari Perin
Design and Production: Kristen Wurz

Library of Congress Cataloging-in-Publication Data
Scones, muffins, and tea cakes : breakfast breads and teatime spreads /
edited and introduction by Heidi Haughy Cusick;
photography by Deborah Jones and Kathryn Kleinman.
p.   cm.
Includes index.
ISBN 0-00-225201-5
1. Baked products.   2. Cakes.   3. Menus   I. Cusick, Heidi Haughy.
TX763.S385   1996
641.8'15–dc20   CIP 95-24699
Printed in China
9 10

Acknowledgments
Collins Publishers would like to thank all the Country Garden Cookbook
authors and photographers; Sandra Cook and Stephanie Greenleigh,
food stylists; Allyson Levy, assistant food stylist; and Michaele Thunen and
Sara Slavin, floral and prop stylists. Special thanks to Sharon Kramis
for developing new recipes for this collection.

CONTENTS

Introduction

Step into a kitchen redolent of hospitality. Scones are cooling on the counter, tea sandwiches and muffins grace the table, and cake spices scent the air. Yeasty aromas fill the room, infusing it with welcome odors. Steam sings from the tea kettle, coffee burbles in its pot. As you and your companions choose their favorite pastries from the enticing display, conversation flows as freely as the hot libations.

A relaxed and entertaining occasion such as this is easy to arrange given the inherent convenience of scones, muffins and tea cakes. Whether baked in the evening or on a day off, these are quick breads which satisfy light or lusty hungers. Scones, muffins and biscuits can be mixed and baked in less than an hour. They freeze well, making it easy to keep on hand a cache of delectables with which to entertain visitors. Accompanying preserves, honeys and spreads may be made in large batches and kept readily available in the refrigerator, freezer or pantry. With the pastries prepared in advance, the only thing left to do when guests arrive is brew the coffee or tea.

Long before the demand for scones and muffins inspired commercial ventures, mornings began with home-baked quickbreads. In this collection, destined to revive tradition, you'll find an inspired variety of easily made pastries to add to your own breakfast and teatime repertoires.

Any event is an excuse for enjoying one of these recipes: A late breakfast or brunch allows you to linger over and enjoy moist Whole Wheat Peach Muffins or flaky Black Currant Cream Biscuits. A pause in the afternoon for a spot of tea and a slice of Tomato Spice Tea Bread is guaranteed to rejuvenate the spirit and restore energy.

Perhaps the occasion calls for a formal afternoon tea, as ritualized in Europe and Asia. Classic open-faced tea sandwiches topped with watercress or Lemon Cucumber Tea Sandwiches will gratify the senses. Round out the menu with more refined canapés, such as those in the Tea Sandwiches chapter, embellished with flowers and herbs, herbaceous honeys, flavored butters or, my favorite, Goat Cheese with Mille Herbes.

Weddings and baby showers, graduations, family reunions, housewarmings and birthdays all create opportunities to gather for tea or coffee and baked tidbits.

These recipes cover an amazing variety of flavors, so it is hard to decide which to try first.

Sweet concoctions are flavored with delicate lavender honey, oranges, black currants and almonds. For those of you who prefer the savory, there are biscuits and breads flecked with black olives, Parmesan cheese, chèvre, rosemary and thyme. Muffins, from classic English to contemporary carrot, from spicy corn to chocolate cherry pecan, cover all flavors.

In the Spreads chapter you'll find a range of sweet and savory toppings offering numerous ways to enliven any freshly baked good. For everyday enjoyment, the herbed honeys, berry jams, and marmalades perk up the plainest toast. And, indispensable for a formal tea are Lemon Curd and Clotted Cream.

To get started, try one of the eight special occasion menus ranging from breakfast for two to tea for twenty. A gathering with a theme, such as a Mexican Fiesta or Mad Hatter's Tea Party, will guarantee a celebratory air and give your party a sense of occasion. The host will have as much fun as the guests. For a more intimate event, set the table with grandmother's tea set when enjoying the company of friends with literary inclinations. You can expect the conversation to become quite lively, and you will soon understand why M.F.K. Fisher said that she didn't drink tea any longer because it made her

"drunk as a skunk." As for the guest list, heed what Henry Fieldings wrote in *Love in Several Masquerades,* "Love and scandal are the best sweeteners of tea." In any case, these menus are designed to inspire your own creativity and spawn the next gathering.

Exploit the versatility of quick breads and spreads. They need not be limited to breakfast and teatime. The Sweet and Spicy Red Onion Marmalade and Tomato Tapenade can top anything from sandwiches to pizza. Likewise Pumpkin and Chutney Kolaches and Savory Zucchini and Cheese Madeleines make appealing appetizers. Skillet Corn Bread served with Jalepeño-Cumin Butter is a zesty alternative to bread and butter at dinner. The Southern Tea Cakes are marvelous bases for strawberry shortcake. And Lemon Squares makes a tantalizing dessert.

Just as the recipes in this collection enhance my repertoire, they deserve a place in yours. Each is an excuse to preheat the oven so that the next person who enters your kitchen will be embraced by the warmth of your own welcoming batch of homey breads and luscious spreads.

SPECIAL OCCASION MENUS

Sunday Morning on the Veranda

Serves 2

"Sunday, sweet Sunday, my one day with you, dreaming the hours away . . ." This song from *Flower Drum Song* has been an inspiration since the first Sunday morning my husband and I spent together. Even today, Sunday morning is a ritual of making breakfast, reading the newspaper, and catching up with each other. On sunny days our favorite place to eat breakfast is on the porch.

This menu offers a pleasant assortment of flavors. To make it work for only two, plan to have leftover coffee cake on Monday, unless friends drop by on Sunday. I bake the spice bread in three tiny loaf pans and freeze them or share them with neighbors. The spicy bite of the red onion marmalade is calmed by the fruit, and the cinnamon complements the Tomato Spice Tea Bread. To broil grapefruit, sprinkle the cut side with sugar and caramelize it under the broiler.

Cherry Pecan Coffee Cake
Tomato Spice Tea Bread
Sweet and Spicy Red Onion Marmalade
Broiled grapefruit
Soft-boiled eggs

A Mother's Day Spring Breakfast

Serves 8 to 10

Bouquets of purple and yellow irises, lace-trimmed napkins, a basket of strawberries and an assortment of pastries begin the celebratory day. Children are encouraged to participate in the preparations. Let the young ones assemble sandwiches and spoon marmalade into serving dishes. The older ones can slice the quick bread, whip the cream, and take the scones out of the oven.

With their homemade cards in hand, the children parade into mom's boudoir with the first berry-topped scone and cup of coffee on a tray. If she loves breakfast in bed, serve the complete menu on a tray. Invite the whole family to fête mom, or at least eight to ten people with a cause to celebrate any special occasion on a lovely spring morning. With fewer celebrants, leftovers will keep you going for days.

Prizewinning Orange Scones with Berries and Cream
Mango and Crystallized Ginger Quick Bread
Apricot and Orange Marmalade
Lemon Sandwiches
Parmesan and Black Pepper Pillows
Parsley and Chive Butter or Tomato Tapenade

Autumn's Bounty Brunch

Serves 20

A weekend brunch with my closest cohorts is a favorite pastime. The balmy days of autumn always signal the time to invite them over to share tales of summer experiences.

This menu features end-of-the-season crops. And the dishes are hearty enough to sustain the biggest eater until dinner. The Tomato Ginger Upside-Down Cake combines two incredibly complementary flavors and offers an opportunity to use up a glut of luscious homegrown tomatoes.

Prepare the herb honey a week before. Bake the muffins in miniature muffin tins so that there will be at least one for everyone. Bake two batches of Parmesan pillows. The kolaches recipe makes twenty-four pastries—double the recipe, depending on your guests' appetites.

Lemon-Glazed Huckleberry Muffins
Zucchini and Black Walnut Bars with
  Cream Cheese Frosting
Tomato Ginger Upside-Down Cake
Pumpkin and Chutney Kolaches
Chèvre and Herbes de Provence Scones
Parmesan and Black Pepper Pillows
Mediterranean Herb Honey
Apple Butter

A Fiesta Breakfast

Serves 10

Fill a piñata with hard fruit-shaped candies, set the table with bold-colored linens, put on some mariachi music, and celebrate the Mexican-American culinary heritage with this menu. Many of the recipes here feature south-of-the-border seasonings such as cumin and cilantro.

For this menu, you need to make one batch each of the biscuits and muffins. Substitute cilantro for the thyme in the biscuits and add a dash or two of chili powder to the dough, if desired. Make one loaf of the squash bread and cut the slices into fourths. Arrange them on a flat basket or Mexican platter. Wrap the tortillas in foil and heat them in the oven to serve with the red onion marmalade. Scramble some eggs with cut-up tortillas and serve them with salsa and sautéed chorizo on the side.

Sun-Dried Tomato Biscuits
Spicy Green Onion Corn Muffins with
  Jalapeño and Cumin Butter
Banana and Butternut Squash Bread
Sweet and Spicy Red Onion Marmalade
  on flour tortillas
Pineapple spears
Scrambled eggs with tortillas
Sautéed chorizo sausage and salsa

A Mad Hatter's Children's Tea Party

Serves 10 to 12

Riddles, hats and pint-sized participants are the requirements for this fun-filled party. A reading from Lewis Carroll's *Alice's Adventures in Wonderland* about the Mad Hatter's tea party is indispensable to set the mood. Inspired by the Hatter, the Dormouse and the March Hare, a game of musical chairs is appropriate. Have the children think up riddles and create imaginative hats.

To get everyone started at teatime, make the English muffins a day in advance. Top them with pizza sauce and cheese and set under the broiler. On a low table, lay out split buttermilk scones (leave out the cranberries). These will be the bases for each child to make into faces using a cream cheese background and other ingredients to make eyes, noses, mouths and hair. Bake the banana bread batter in miniature muffin tins. Serve herb tea in petite or full-sized teacups.

Classic English Muffin pizzas
Buttermilk Breakfast Scones
Face makings: cream cheese with Mille Herbes,
*   raisins, grated carrots, sprouts and sliced olives*
Banana and Butternut Squash Bread
Chunky Chocolate Cherry Pecan Muffin Cakes
Herb teas

A Literary Tea

Serves 8 to 10

If Marcel Proust had madeleines at tea, what would Gertrude Stein and Alice B. Toklas, Anaïs Nin and Henry Miller, M.F.K. Fisher and Anthelme Brillat-Savarin have if they had taken tea with me? Choosing from this collection, I came up with the following menu to serve in their honor, or at a tea in which to celebrate your favorite author's birthday or literary masterpiece.

My chosen authors would undoubtedly appreciate the essence of madeleines, especially if they were savory, quichelike and filled with understated ingredients. (Make only half the recipe.) Likewise, the practicality of overnight rolls, which are filled with the concentrated richness of onions, is perfect. Garden Sage Honey adds the right herb to the lofty theme. For dessert, typical American cakes are out. M.F.K. blatantly condemned them, and I could find no particular love for cakes reflected by the works of the others. Instead serve a platter of seasonal fruit and cheese.

Savory Zucchini and Cheese Madeleines
Onion Confit Overnight Breakfast Rolls
Black Olive and Rosemary Scones
Garden Sage Honey
Seasonal fruit and cheese platter

An After-Ski Tea

Serves 8

As soon as the boots hit the porch, the snow is brushed off the hats, and the jackets and gloves are hooked next to the fireplace, skiers are ready for something to eat after a day on the slopes. Hot tea and a snack are just the thing.

In minutes, the water in the tea kettle is rolling to a boil, muffins and scones are warming in the oven, and the gang is settled around the table with tales of valor and humor, near disasters and hair-raising adventures. The kolaches are moist pumpkin-infused pastry drops topped with chutney you can make in the morning. The marmalade is also made in advance, and a daily dose is required so that everyone is fortified with a measure of vitamin C. The dried fruit in the muffins is iron-rich and energy replacing. Except for the kolaches, which are best eaten right away, the muffins and biscuits keep well, and one recipe of each made in advance can feed eight after-ski noshers for three days.

Carrot Muffins with Raisins and Dried Pineapple
Chunky Chocolate Cherry Pecan Muffin Cakes
Apricot and Orange Marmalade
Pumpkin and Chutney Kolaches
Black Currant Cream Biscuits

A Victorian Christmas Tea

Serves 20

A high-ceilinged room lit with tiny white lights sets the scene. Pine bough garlands tied with velvet bows over the fireplace and along the wainscoting embellish the decor. The gentlemen are invited to wear suits and the women to dress in high-necked ruffled blouses and long skirts. Someone reads from a volume of Dickens.

In the center of a marble buffet, the tea service reigns. Dainty sandwiches topped with lemon, cucumber, watercress, smoked salmon and Tomato Tapenade are passed. Cranberry scones are split and eaten with Clotted Cream and Cranberry Butter. Make one and a half recipes of the scones, cut the tea cake into 20 slices, double the Lemon Cucumber Tea Sandwich recipe and make at least 40 other canapés topped with goat cheese, Tomato Tapenade and slivers of smoked salmon.

Buttermilk Breakfast Scones with Dried Cranberries
Almond Tea Cake
Cranberry Butter
Clotted Cream
Lemon Cucumber Tea Sandwiches
Open-Faced Watercress Sandwiches
Canapés with Goat Cheese with Mille Herbes,
   Tomato Tapenade and smoked salmon

Scones & Biscuits

For breakfast, teatime or even supper, scones and biscuits are the age-old favorites of the quick breads, and for good reason. Whether prepared from a basic dough or flavored with herbs and other seasonings, when split in half, these make the most practical as well as the most versatile, flaky and delicious bases for the toppings of your desire.

Scones and biscuits are basically made the same way. Scones are a little richer than biscuits because eggs, and sometimes cream, are included. Typically, biscuit dough is dropped on a baking sheet or rolled out and cut into rounds, while the dough for scones is patted into big rounds and cut into wedge shapes. In this chapter, I've also included recipes that depart from the traditional forms, such as the Prizewinning Orange Scones, which are rolled up like jelly rolls and the Sun-Dried Tomato Biscuits, which are cut into squares.

Personalize your scones and biscuits to suit your own fancy. The secret to making them light and flaky is to work the dough as little as possible but just enough to activate the gluten in the flour.

Prizewinning Orange Scones with Berries and Cream

With or without the berries and cream, these orange-zested rolled-up scones are classics.
Try them with one of the marmalades in the Spreads chapter.

Scones:
2 cups sifted all-purpose flour
1 tablespoon baking powder
1 teaspoon salt
2 tablespoons granulated sugar
5 1/2 tablespoons unsalted butter, chilled and
*   cut into pieces*
1 extra large egg, beaten
1/2 cup heavy (whipping) cream
2 tablespoons unsalted butter, melted

1/2 cup granulated sugar
1 tablespoon orange zest

6 to 8 cups fresh berries (such as strawberries,
*   raspberries, blackberries and tayberries), washed*
*   and dried*
3/4 to 1 cup granulated sugar, depending upon the
*   sweetness of the berries*
1 to 1 1/2 cups heavy (whipping) cream, whipped
*   and lightly sweetened with 2 teaspoons of*
*   granulated sugar*

Preheat the oven to 425 degrees F. Lightly grease a baking sheet and set aside.

In a small bowl, stir together the flour, baking powder, salt and sugar. Using a pastry blender, 2 knives, or your fingertips, cut the butter into the dry ingredients until it resembles coarse cornmeal. In a small bowl, combine the egg and cream and add to the flour mixture. Mix until just blended together.

Turn out the batter onto a lightly floured board and knead for 1 minute. Roll dough into a rectangle approximately 4 inches by 8 inches.

Brush the dough with the melted butter.

Sprinkle with the sugar and orange zest. Roll up, jelly-roll fashion, and seal the long seam by pinching it together lightly with your fingers.

Cut the roll into eight 1-inch-thick slices. Lay slices down sideways on the prepared baking sheet and bake for 12 to 15 minutes, or until scones are golden.

Slice the strawberries and place in a large pretty bowl with other whole berries, if available. Sprinkle with sugar and refrigerate for 1 to 2 hours. To serve, heap spoonfuls of berries over each scone and top with freshly whipped cream.
Makes 8 scones

Lemon Scones

*At teatime, serve these lemon-scented scones with Lemon Curd or Meyer Lemon Marmalade
and a little Clotted Cream, if you are a traditionalist. (photo p. 12)*

2 cups all-purpose flour
2 tablespoons granulated sugar
2 tablespoons baking powder
Zest of 2 lemons, finely diced
2 tablespoons unsalted butter, chilled and
    cut into small pieces

2 eggs, lightly beaten
$1/2$ cup heavy (whipping) cream
$3/4$ cup currants
1 egg beaten with 1 tablespoon cold water,
    for egg wash

Preheat the oven to 400 degrees F. Lightly grease a baking sheet and set aside.

Sift the flour, sugar and baking powder into a large mixing bowl. Add the zest and rub the butter into the flour by hand or cut in with a pastry blender. Combine the eggs and cream and blend into the flour mixture. Fold in the currants. Do not overmix.

Gather the dough into a ball and divide in half. On a lightly floured surface, roll into 2 circles $1/2$ inch thick. Using a 2-inch round cookie cutter, cut the dough into scones. Press together leftover dough, roll into a circle $1/2$ inch thick and continue cutting out rounds until all the dough is used.

Place the scones 2 inches apart on 2 baking sheets and refrigerate for 15 minutes. Brush the tops of the scones with the egg wash and bake for 15 to 20 minutes, or until golden brown. *Makes approximately 24 scones*

Buttermilk Breakfast Scones with Dried Cranberries

These tender, traditionally shaped scones are updated with dried cranberries and are made without eggs. They are delicious served warm with Cranberry Butter.

3 cups unbleached all-purpose flour
^{1}/$_3$ cup granulated sugar
2 ^{1}/$_2$ teaspoons baking powder
^{1}/$_2$ teaspoon baking soda
^{3}/$_4$ teaspoon salt
^{3}/$_4$ cup (1 ^{1}/$_2$ sticks) chilled margarine,
    cut into 6 to 8 pieces

^{3}/$_4$ cup dried cranberries
1 teaspoon grated orange zest
1 cup buttermilk

Glaze:
1 tablespoon heavy cream
^{1}/$_4$ teaspoon ground cinnamon
2 tablespoons granulated sugar

Preheat the oven to 400 degrees F. Lightly grease a baking sheet and set aside.

In a large bowl, stir the flour, sugar, baking powder, baking soda and salt. Add the margarine and beat with an electric mixer until well blended. Add the dried cranberries and orange zest. Pour in the buttermilk and mix until blended.

Gather the dough into a ball and divide in half. On a lightly floured board, roll into 2 circles, approximately ^{1}/$_2$ to ^{3}/$_4$ inch thick. Cut each circle into 8 wedges.

To make the glaze, in a small bowl, combine the cream, cinnamon and sugar. Set aside.

Bake the scones on the prepared baking sheet for 12 to 15 minutes, or until they are golden. Remove scones from the oven and brush with the glaze. *Makes 16 scones*

Black Olive and Rosemary Scones

*Serve these hearty scones as an accompaniment to a light lunch.
To complement the olives even more, try them topped with Tomato Tapenade.*

3 cups all-purpose flour
1 tablespoon granulated sugar
2 1/2 teaspoons baking powder
1/2 teaspoon baking soda
1/2 teaspoon salt
3/4 cup (1 1/2 sticks) unsalted butter, chilled and
    cut into 1/2-inch slices

1/2 cup pitted Kalamata olives, cut into
    thirds crosswise
2 teaspoons finely chopped fresh rosemary
2 teaspoons grated lemon zest
1 cup buttermilk
1 egg beaten with 1 tablespoon cold water, for egg wash
2 teaspoons coarse sea salt

Preheat the oven to 400 degrees F. Lightly grease a baking sheet and set aside.

In a large bowl, stir together the flour, sugar, baking powder, baking soda and salt. With the tips of your fingers, blend the butter into the flour mixture until it resembles coarse cornmeal. Stir in the olives, rosemary and lemon zest. Make a well in the center of the mixture and add the buttermilk. With a fork, mix until well blended.

Gather the dough into a ball and divide in half. On a lightly floured board, roll into 2 circles 1/2 inch thick. Brush each circle with the egg wash and sprinkle each with 1 teaspoon of the sea salt. With a sharp knife, cut each circle into 6 triangle-shaped wedges.

Bake the scones on the prepared baking sheet for 20 to 25 minutes, or until golden brown.
Makes 12 scones

Chèvre and Herbes de Provence Scones

These scones are perfect served with Goat Cheese with Mille Herbs,
Herb Flower Butter, or Mediterranean Herb Honey.

1 ¹/2 cups all-purpose flour
¹/2 cup whole-wheat flour
2 teaspoons baking powder
¹/2 teaspoon baking soda
1 tablespoon herbes de Provence
³/4 teaspoon salt

1 tablespoon brown sugar
¹/2 cup (1 stick) unsalted butter, chilled and
    cut into ¹/2-inch slices
3 ounces chèvre (goat cheese), broken into small pieces
1 egg, beaten
²/3 cup buttermilk

Preheat the oven to 400 degrees F. Lightly grease a baking sheet and set aside.

In a large bowl, stir together the flours, baking powder, baking soda, *herbes de Provence*, salt and brown sugar. With the tips of your fingers, blend the butter into the flour mixture until it resembles coarse cornmeal. Gently stir in the chèvre.

In a small bowl, mix together the egg and buttermilk. Make a well in the center of the flour mixture and add the wet ingredients, stirring until completely blended together.

Gather the dough into a ball and divide in half. (The dough will be very moist.) On a floured board, roll into 2 circles ¹/2 inch thick. Cut each circle into 6 wedges.

Bake the scones on the prepared baking sheet for 20 to 25 minutes, or until golden brown. *Makes 12 scones*

Parmesan and Black Pepper Pillows

These delicious cheese-topped biscuits puff up like little pillows.
Serve them drizzled with Garden Sage Honey.

2 cups self-rising flour
1 tablespoon granulated sugar
2 teaspoons baking powder
$^1/_2$ teaspoon freshly ground black pepper

$^1/_3$ cup shortening
$^1/_2$ cup grated Parmesan cheese, plus $^1/_4$ cup,
    for topping
1 cup buttermilk

Preheat the oven to 400 degrees F. Lightly grease a baking sheet and set aside.

In a bowl, stir together the flour, sugar, baking powder and pepper. With an electric hand-held mixer, blend in the shortening, being careful not to overmix. Make a well in the center of the mixture and, using a fork, stir in the $^1/_2$ cup Parmesan cheese and the buttermilk. Mix just until blended.

Gather the dough into a ball. On a lightly floured board, roll out into a circle $^1/_2$ inch thick. With a 2-inch round biscuit cutter, cut 10 to 12 rounds. Press together the leftover dough, roll into a circle $^1/_2$ inch thick and continue cutting out rounds until all the dough is used.

Place the biscuits on the prepared baking sheet and sprinkle each biscuit with a teaspoon of grated Parmesan cheese. Bake for 18 to 20 minutes, or until golden brown. *Makes 12 biscuits*

Sun-Dried Tomato Biscuits

These biscuits can stand alone or be topped with herbed butter. Leave out the tomatoes and thyme and you have a delectably basic biscuit.

2 cups unbleached white flour
1 tablespoon baking powder
1 tablespoon granulated sugar
1 teaspoon salt
$^1/_2$ cup (1 stick) unsalted butter, frozen
2 eggs
$^1/_2$ cup buttermilk
$^1/_3$ cup sun-dried tomatoes, finely chopped
1 tablespoon finely chopped fresh thyme

Preheat the oven to 400 degrees F. Lightly oil a baking sheet and set aside.

In a large bowl, sift together the dry ingredients. Finely chop the butter. By hand or in a food processor, blend with the dry ingredients. The mixture should not be thoroughly blended, but should have pea-sized clumps of butter and flour.

In a small bowl, whisk the eggs and buttermilk together. Stir in the sun-dried tomatoes and thyme. Using the pulse of the food processor or just your hands, work together the dry and moist ingredients until the dough begins to come together. Do not overwork or biscuits will be tough.

Turn the dough onto a floured board and roll to $^1/_2$-inch thickness. Fold in half and roll out again. Fold in half again and roll to $^3/_4$-inch thickness. Cut the dough into 2-inch-square biscuits. Transfer to the baking sheet and bake for 12 minutes, or until fluffy and brown. *Makes 12 biscuits*

Lavender Honey and Sweet Fennel Biscuits

The licorice undertones of the fennel complement the lavender honey in these square tea biscuits. Try making your own lavender honey, using the recipe for flavored honey in the Spreads chapter.

2 cups self-rising flour
3 tablespoons unsalted butter
3 tablespoons shortening
1 tablespoon fennel seed
$^3/_4$ cup ice water
3 tablespoons lavender honey

Preheat the oven to 425 degrees F. Lightly grease a baking sheet and set aside.

Place the flour in a large bowl. With the tips of your fingers, blend in the butter and shortening until it resembles coarse cornmeal. Stir in the fennel seeds.

Make a well in the center of the flour mixture and stir in the water and honey until blended. Gather the dough into a ball.

On a lightly floured board, roll out the dough into a rectangle $^1/_2$ inch thick. With a sharp knife, cut the dough into small rectangles 1 $^1/_2$ inches by 2 inches. Transfer to the prepared baking sheet and bake for 12 to 15 minutes, or until lightly golden brown. Serve warm, drizzled with more honey. *Makes 18 biscuits*

Left to right: Sun-Dried Tomato Biscuits and Tomato Spice Tea Bread (recipe p. 55)

Black Currant Cream Biscuits

This is a perfect little tea biscuit.
Serve with Clotted Cream and a dollop of fresh jam.

2 cups all-purpose flour
2 tablespoons granulated sugar
1 tablespoon baking powder
¹/₂ teaspoon salt
¹/₃ cup unsalted butter, chilled and cut into
    ¹/₂-inch slices

¹/₂ cup dried black currants
1 cup heavy (whipping) cream

Glaze:
1 tablespoon heavy (whipping) cream
¹/₄ teaspoon ground cinnamon
2 tablespoons granulated sugar

Preheat the oven to 450 degrees F. Lightly grease a baking sheet and set aside.

In a large bowl, stir together the flour, sugar, baking powder and salt. With the tips of your fingers, blend the butter into the flour mixture until it resembles coarse cornmeal. Add the black currants. Pour in the whipping cream and mix until blended.

Gather the dough into a ball. On a lightly floured board, roll into a circle ³/₄ inch thick.

Using a 2-inch scallop-edged biscuit cutter, cut out 8 circles. Press together the leftover dough, roll into a circle ³/₄ inch thick and cut 2 to 3 more biscuits.

To make the glaze, in a small bowl, whisk together the cream, cinnamon and sugar until blended. Set aside.

Place the biscuits, 2 inches apart, on the prepared baking sheet and bake for 15 minutes or until golden. Remove from the oven and lightly brush with the glaze. *Makes 10 to 12 biscuits*

Muffins

A morning without muffins is like a bird without song, a garden without flowers, an oven without heat. Simply saying "muffins" sings their praises and brings to mind the moist warmth of tender domes in their tins removed piping hot from the oven.

In my house, muffins are inspired on an almost daily basis by overripe bananas from the kitchen counter, raspberries from the garden picked before breakfast, huckleberries in the freezer, or a box of cornmeal in the pantry. From beginning to end, it takes less than an hour to have muffins on the table. Doubling the recipe is an expedient way to make sure muffins are always on hand for breakfast, tea, supper or a snack because they freeze so well.

The best muffins come from the least amount of work. When mixing the batter, gently stir the liquids into the dry ingredients and mix until just blended. This produces light muffins that rise evenly. Overmixing will make them rubbery.

Whole Wheat Peach Muffins

In this moist, golden muffin, puréed peaches replace some of the oil and liquids, and chunks of peach intensify the fruity flavor. For a sweeter taste, sprinkle the tops with sugar.

4 peaches (approximately 1 3/4 pounds)
1 cup whole-wheat flour, preferably stone-ground
1 1/2 cups all-purpose flour
1 tablespoon baking powder
1/2 teaspoon baking soda
2/3 cup firmly packed dark brown sugar

1/2 teaspoon ground cinnamon
1 teaspoon ground ginger
1/4 teaspoon salt
1/4 cup safflower oil
1 large egg
4 teaspoons granulated sugar (optional)

Preheat the oven to 400 degrees F. Grease 8 standard-size muffin cups or 2 miniature muffin tins. Set aside.

Peel 3 of the peaches, then pit and cut into chunks. Purée them in a food processor or blender. Cut the remaining peach, unpeeled, into 1/2-inch pieces. Set aside.

In a large mixing bowl, combine the flours, baking powder, baking soda, brown sugar, cinnamon, ginger and salt. Make a well in the center and pour in the peach purée, oil and egg.

Stir just until moistened and then fold in the chopped peaches.

Fill each muffin cup with batter to the top. Sprinkle the sugar over the batter, if desired, before baking. Bake in the center of the oven for 25 to 30 minutes for regular muffins or 20 to 25 minutes for mini-muffins, or until a toothpick inserted in the center comes out clean and the tops are cracked. Remove from the pan and cool completely. *Makes 8 regular or 24 miniature muffins*

Blueberry Banana Muffins

These moist muffins are full of plump, juicy blueberries and impart a background flavor of banana.

$^1/_2$ cup (1 stick) margarine
$^3/_4$ cup granulated sugar
2 eggs
1 cup mashed bananas (2 to 3 ripe bananas)
$^1/_2$ cup milk
2 cups all-purpose flour
2 teaspoons baking powder
$^1/_2$ teaspoon ground cinnamon
2 cups fresh or frozen blueberries

Preheat the oven to 375 degrees F. Grease one standard-size 12-cup muffin tin and set aside.

In a medium bowl with an electric mixer, cream the margarine and sugar. Add the eggs, one at a time. Mix in the bananas and milk.

In another mixing bowl, combine the flour, baking powder and cinnamon. Add the margarine mixture to the dry ingredients and mix only until the batter is moist. Do not overmix.

Carefully stir in the whole blueberries. If you are using frozen blueberries, add them to your recipe while they are still frozen or they will turn your batter purple. Spoon the batter into the muffin cups, filling the cups to the top. Bake in the oven for 30 to 35 minutes, or until muffins are golden brown.

Let cool for 5 minutes in the muffin tin, then transfer to a cooling rack. The muffins can be stored in a tightly sealed plastic container or in plastic bags. *Makes 12 muffins*

Lemon-Glazed Huckleberry Muffins

These muffins call for tart, plump huckleberries, but you can use blueberries instead.

$^1/_2$ cup corn oil
2 eggs
1 cup granulated sugar
1 tablespoon lemon zest
2 tablespoons fresh lemon juice
$1^3/_4$ cups all-purpose flour
2 teaspoons baking powder
$^1/_2$ teaspoon baking soda
$^1/_2$ teaspoon salt
$1^1/_2$ cups huckleberries

Lemon Glaze:
$^1/_4$ cup powdered sugar
2 teaspoons lemon zest
2 tablespoons fresh lemon juice

Preheat the oven to 375 degrees F. Grease one standard-size 12-cup muffin tin and set aside.

In a large bowl with an electric mixer, beat the corn oil and eggs until well blended. Add the sugar and continue beating for 2 minutes, or until the mixture is creamy. Add lemon zest and lemon juice.

In a small bowl, combine the flour, baking powder, baking soda and salt. Using a wooden spoon, stir all dry ingredients into the creamy mixture. Be careful not to overmix.

Using a rubber spatula, gently fold in the huckleberries. Spoon the batter into the muffin cups until they are three-quarters full. Bake in

the oven for 25 minutes, or until muffins are golden brown.

While the muffins are baking, prepare the lemon glaze. In a small bowl, combine the powdered sugar, lemon zest and lemon juice. Stir and set aside.

Remove the muffin tin from the oven and pierce each muffin 6 to 8 times with a skewer. Spoon the lemon glaze over the muffins while they are still warm. Let sit for 5 minutes, then remove the muffins from the pan. *Makes 12 muffins*

Chunky Chocolate Cherry Pecan Muffin Cakes

Bake these in the new muffin "tops only" baking tins or miniature muffin tins, and you'll end up with wonderful miniature cakes you can eat in small bites. For the chocolate lover in your life, bake them in shallow heart-shaped individual cake molds.

$^1/_2$ cup (1 stick) butter
$^3/_4$ cup light brown sugar
2 eggs
1 $^3/_4$ cups all-purpose flour
2 teaspoons baking powder
$^1/_2$ teaspoon baking soda
1 cup buttermilk
$^1/_2$ cup dried cherries

$^1/_3$ cup chopped pecans
2 ounces ($^1/_2$ cup) semisweet chocolate, chopped into
    $^1/_4$-inch pieces

Glaze:
$^1/_4$ cup powdered sugar
1 tablespoon water
$^1/_2$ teaspoon vanilla extract

Preheat the oven to 375 degrees F.

In a bowl with an electric mixer on medium speed, beat the butter until creamy. Add the brown sugar and continue beating until blended. Add the eggs, one at a time, and continue mixing, blending each egg into the butter mixture.

In a small bowl, mix together the flour, baking powder and baking soda. With a wooden spoon, stir half of the flour mixture into the wet ingredients. Then stir in the buttermilk, being careful not to overmix. Carefully fold in the remaining flour mixture, cherries, pecans and chocolate.

Drop the batter by spoonfuls into ungreased muffin tops pan. Bake for 20 minutes. Let cool for 5 minutes in the pan.

To make the glaze, in a small bowl, mix together the powdered sugar, water and vanilla until smooth.

With a rubber spatula, drizzle approximately 1 tablespoon of the glaze over each muffin top. Remove from the pan and serve. *Makes 6 large or 12 small muffin tops*

Kabocha Corn Muffins with Sweet Onions

Moist and tender, these easy-to-make muffins are perfect for brunch or high tea.
Mashed pumpkin, butternut, buttercup, acorn or Hubbard squash can replace the kabocha.

1 1/2 cups coarse-grind yellow cornmeal
1/2 cup all-purpose flour
1 1/2 teaspoons baking powder
1 teaspoon baking soda
1 teaspoon salt
1 tablespoon chopped fresh sage or
   1/2 teaspoon dried, crumbled

1 teaspoon chopped fresh rosemary or
   1/4 teaspoon dried, crumbled
1 small Vidalia or other sweet onion, finely diced
2 large eggs
3/4 cup sour cream or plain yogurt
4 tablespoons (1/2 stick) unsalted butter, melted
1 cup cooked and mashed kabocha squash

Preheat the oven to 425 degrees F. Grease one standard-size 12-cup or two miniature muffin tins and set aside.

In a large bowl, stir together the cornmeal, flour, baking powder, baking soda, salt, sage and rosemary. Stir in the onion and set aside.

In a second bowl, beat the eggs lightly, then stir in the sour cream and melted butter. Whisk in the squash until smooth.

Add the squash mixture to the cornmeal mixture and stir to combine fully.

Spoon the batter into the muffin cups until each cup is two-thirds full. Bake in the oven 20 to 25 minutes, or until golden brown and a toothpick inserted in the center comes out clean. Let cool a few minutes, then turn out of the tins and serve hot. *Makes 12 regular or 24 miniature muffins*

Spicy Green Onion Corn Muffins

*These muffins are moist and flavorful and make a splendid addition
to a breakfast of chorizo, scrambled eggs and salsa.*

1 cup buttermilk
$^1/_4$ cup firmly packed brown sugar
$^1/_4$ cup sour cream
1 egg
$^1/_4$ cup vegetable oil
$^3/_4$ cup blue or yellow medium-grind cornmeal
1 $^1/_4$ cups unbleached white flour
2 teaspoons baking powder
$^1/_2$ teaspoon baking soda

$^1/_4$ teaspoon salt
1 tablespoon pure ground chili powder (ancho or
 chipotle)
$^1/_3$ cup finely chopped green onion, including
 the tender green tops
$^1/_4$ cup grated red onion
$^3/_4$ cup grated Monterey Jack cheese
$^1/_2$ cup chopped fresh cilantro

Preheat the oven to 400 degrees F. Grease one standard-size 12-cup or two miniature muffin tins.

In a large bowl, beat together the buttermilk, brown sugar, sour cream, egg and oil until well blended. In a medium-size bowl, stir together the cornmeal, flour, baking powder, baking soda, salt and chili powder. Gradually add the flour mixture to the buttermilk mixture, stirring until blended. Fold in the green onion, red onion, cheese and cilantro.

Divide the batter among the muffin cups, filling each one three-fourths full. Bake for 15 minutes, or until browned and firm to the touch. Let cool in the pan briefly, then turn out of the pan onto a cooling rack. Serve warm. *Makes 12 regular or 24 miniature muffins*

Carrot Muffins with Raisins and Dried Pineapple

Now you can have carrot cake in muffin shapes! Bursting with carrots, pecans,
raisins and tart dried pineapple, these are nutritiously good for breakfast or a snack anytime.

3 eggs
3/4 cup buttermilk
3/4 cup canola oil
1 cup honey
1 teaspoon vanilla extract
3 cups grated carrots
1 cup raisins

1/2 cup (2 ounces) chopped pecans
3/4 cup chopped dried pineapple
1 cup whole-wheat flour
1 1/2 cups all-purpose flour
2 teaspoons baking soda
2 teaspoons ground cinnamon
1/2 teaspoon salt

Preheat the oven to 375 degrees F. Grease three standard-size 6-cup muffin tins and set aside.

In a large bowl, beat the eggs with a wire whisk. Add buttermilk, oil, honey and vanilla and mix together until well blended.

With a wooden spoon, stir in the carrots, raisins, pecans and pineapple.

In a small bowl, mix together the flours, baking soda, cinnamon and salt. Gently fold the dry ingredients into the carrot mixture and mix until just blended.

Spoon the batter into the muffin cups, filling the cups to the top. Bake for 25 minutes, or until the muffins spring back when lightly pressed with your fingertips. Let cool for 5 minutes in the muffin tins, then transfer to a cooling rack. *Makes 18 muffins*

Classic English Muffins

You'll need English muffin or egg-poaching rings to make these old favorites.
They are made from a yeasted dough, so they take time to prepare, but are worth the effort.
If you start them right after lunch, they'll be ready for teatime. Serve them with soft butter
and sweet toppings like Strawberry Jam or the savory Tomato Tapenade.

1 package (scant 1 tablespoon) active dry yeast,
    dissolved in 2 tablespoons warm water
1 tablespoon granulated sugar
$^1/_2$ cup warm water
$^3/_4$ cup warm milk

2 teaspoons salt
3 $^1/_2$ cups all-purpose flour
$^1/_4$ teaspoon baking soda, dissolved in 1 tablespoon
    warm water
3 tablespoons unsalted butter, at room temperature

In a large bowl, combine the yeast mixture, sugar, water, milk and salt and stir until well blended. Add in 2 cups of flour and, using a wooden spoon, stir until the batter is well mixed, stretchy and sticky. Cover and let rise for 1 hour.

Add the dissolved baking soda, butter and the remaining 1 $^1/_2$ cups flour to the batter and stir vigorously with a wooden spoon.

Preheat the oven to 350 degrees F. Place 8 buttered 3 $^1/_2$-inch nonstick muffin rings on a lightly greased baking sheet. Spoon the batter into the rings, filling them half full. Let stand until the dough has doubled and fills the muffin rings, approximately 30 minutes.

Place the baking sheet with the muffins in the oven and bake for 15 minutes. Then, with a spatula, lift the filled rings and flip them over. Continue to bake for 5 more minutes.

Remove from the oven. Using a spatula, transfer the muffins, still in their rings, to a cooling rack. Let them sit for at least 10 minutes before slicing.

Remove the rings and slice each muffin in half with a bread knife. If desired, toast them before spreading with your favorite topping. *Makes 8 muffins*

Tea Cakes & Breads

"Whence could it have come to me this all-powerful joy? I was conscious that it was connected with the taste of tea and cake . . ." Of course the cake to which Marcel Proust was referring in *Swann's Way* was the dainty scalloped madeleine, made eternally revered by these very words and the rest of his tea allegory.

One of the primary reasons for having a mug of coffee or a cup of tea is to wash down some delightful morsel, and these tea cakes and breads fill the bill. Many of them have particular appeal for lovers of fresh produce. Some make use of abundant squash, such as the Savory Zucchini and Cheese Madeleines and Banana and Butternut Squash Bread with Mace and Pecans. Others feature seasonal fruit as in the Cherry Pecan Coffee Cake, and Lemon Squares.

I recommend making at least one sweet and one savory recipe for any occasion. That way, whatever the libation, be it strong coffee or an herb-flavored tea, guests have the opportunity to mix flavors according to their own personal tastes.

Cherry Pecan Coffee Cake

Weekend mornings deserve special breakfasts, and this fragrant quick bread makes them so.
To save yourself time in the morning, prepare the topping the night before.

Topping:
3/4 cup pecan halves
4 tablespoons (1/2 stick) unsalted butter, melted
1/2 cup all-purpose flour
2/3 cup firmly packed dark brown sugar
1/2 teaspoon cinnamon
3/4 pound (approximately 2 cups) dark sweet
*   cherries, pitted*

8 tablespoons (1 stick) unsalted butter
1/2 cup granulated sugar
1 large egg
1/2 cup plain low-fat yogurt
1 1/2 teaspoons vanilla extract
1 1/2 cups all-purpose flour
2 teaspoons baking powder
1/2 teaspoon baking soda
1/2 teaspoon salt

Preheat the oven to 350 degrees F. Butter a 9-inch quiche dish or square baking pan. Set aside.

Spread the pecans on a baking sheet and bake for 15 minutes, or until lightly toasted.

In another bowl, stir together the pecans and the remaining topping ingredients. Set aside.

In a large mixing bowl, cream together the butter and sugar with a hand mixer until smooth. Beat in the egg, yogurt and vanilla until well combined. In a small bowl, stir together the flour, baking powder, baking soda and salt, then add to the butter mixture, stirring until just incorporated. The batter will be stiff and very sticky.

Raise the heat to 375 degrees F. Spread the batter evenly over the bottom of the quiche dish. Crumble the cherry topping over the batter and bake in the center of the oven for 35 to 40 minutes until golden brown and the center does not jiggle when lightly shaken. Let cool on a rack.
Serves 6 to 8

Almond Tea Cake

*This is an almond lovers delight and a must
with any formal or informal tea. In the summertime,
garnish it with fresh berries.*

1 cup (2 sticks) unsalted butter
³/4 cup granulated sugar
1 egg, separated
3 ¹/2 ounces almond paste
1 teaspoon almond extract
2 cups sifted, all-purpose flour
¹/2 cup sliced almonds

Preheat the oven to 350 degrees F.

In a bowl with an electric mixer, cream the
butter and sugar. Add the egg yolk, almond paste
and almond extract. Then add the flour and mix
until just blended.

Press the cake batter into an 8-inch ungreased
cake pan (it will seem crumbly, so spread the batter
with your fingertips until level).

In a small bowl, beat the egg white until
foamy. With the back of a metal spoon, spread
the beaten egg white over the cake. Sprinkle
evenly with the sliced almonds. Bake for 30
minutes, or until golden brown. Let cool for 15
minutes, then cut into 8 wedges. *Serves 8*

Southern Tea Cakes

*Served on afternoons throughout the South,
these are a cross between shortbread and pound cake.*

2 cups granulated sugar
1 cup (2 sticks) butter
3 eggs, lightly beaten
³/4 cup buttermilk
1 ¹/2 teaspoons vanilla extract
5 to 6 cups unbleached flour
¹/2 teaspoon freshly grated nutmeg
2 teaspoons baking powder
¹/4 teaspoon baking soda

Preheat the oven to 350 degrees F. Line a rimmed
baking sheet with parchment paper and oil lightly.

In a mixing bowl with a hand or electric
mixer, beat together the sugar and butter until
creamy. Beat in the eggs, buttermilk and vanilla.
In another bowl, combine 2 cups of the flour
with the nutmeg, baking powder and baking soda.
Stir into the batter and mix well. Add another
2 cups of flour and mix well. Beat in enough of
the remaining flour to make a fairly firm dough.

Turn the dough out into the prepared sheet
and pat the dough to distribute it evenly. Dip a
sharp knife into flour and cut through the dough
to make 20 rectangles, 4 cuts one way and 5 the
other. This won't separate the dough, but it will
score it for removal after baking.

Bake for 25 to 30 minutes until puffed and
lightly golden. Do not allow the cakes to brown.
Let cool in the pan, then cut along the scored
lines to separate the cakes. *Makes 20 tea cakes*

Lemon Squares

Lemon squares are addictive confections that can be eaten at any time of the day.

Crust:
3 ¹/₂ cups all-purpose flour
¹/₄ cup confectioners' sugar
¹/₄ teaspoon salt
1 ³/₄ cups (3 ¹/₂ sticks) unsalted butter, cut into
small pieces

Filling:
6 large eggs
2 to 3 cups granulated sugar
1 tablespoon grated lemon zest
¹/₂ cup lemon juice
²/₃ cup all-purpose flour
1 teaspoon baking powder

Confectioners' sugar, for dusting

Preheat the oven to 350 degrees F.

To prepare the crust, in a large bowl, sift together the flour, sugar and salt. With a pastry blender or 2 knives, cut the butter into the flour mixture until it resembles coarse cornmeal. Press the dough into a 17-by-12-by-1-inch baking sheet. Bake for 15 minutes, or until the crust is lightly browned.

To make the filling, in a large bowl with an electric mixer, beat the eggs until blended, then beat in the sugar. Add the zest and gradually fold in the lemon juice. Sift the flour and baking powder into the egg mixture and blend until smooth.

Pour the mixture over the crust and bake for 25 minutes. Let cool in the pan on a rack. Using a sharp knife, carefully cut into squares and dust with confectioners' sugar. *Makes 4 dozen squares*

Zucchini and Black Walnut Bars with Cream Cheese Frosting

*Moist and chewy, these easy bar cookies owe their texture to zucchini and their haunting
flavor to black walnuts. If you can't find black walnuts in a health-food store or specialty market,
try pecans or regular walnuts. Grated winter squash can fill in for the zucchini.*

1 1/2 cups loosely packed, coarsely grated zucchini
2 large eggs
1 cup granulated sugar
3/4 cup corn oil
1 1/2 teaspoons vanilla extract
1 1/2 cups all-purpose flour
1 teaspoon baking powder
1/2 teaspoon salt
1 teaspoon ground cinnamon

1/2 teaspoon ground allspice
1/4 teaspoon freshly grated nutmeg
1 cup black walnuts, coarsely chopped

Frosting:
3 ounces cream cheese, softened
Approximately 2 cups sifted confectioners' sugar
2 tablespoons milk
Dash of salt
1 teaspoon vanilla extract

Preheat the oven to 350 degrees F. Lightly oil
a 9-by-13-inch baking dish and set aside.

Place the zucchini in a colander to drain,
pressing out as much moisture as possible, and
set aside.

In a large bowl and using a wooden spoon,
beat together the eggs, sugar and oil until well
blended. Beat in the vanilla.

In a small bowl, stir together the flour, baking powder, salt, cinnamon, allspice and nutmeg.
Stir the flour mixture into the egg mixture, blending well. Add the zucchini and walnuts and mix
well. Spread into the baking dish.

Bake for 30 minutes, or until the top springs
back when lightly pressed. Let cool completely
on a rack.

To make the frosting, in a bowl and using a
wooden spoon or an electric mixer set on medium speed, beat the cream cheese until smooth.
Then beat in the sugar and milk, adding just
enough sugar to form a spreadable consistency.
Stir in the salt and vanilla until well mixed.

Spread the frosting over the cooled cake.
Using a sharp knife, carefully cut into bars, cutting lengthwise into 4 strips and then across into
8 strips. *Makes 32 bars*

Tomato Ginger Upside-Down Cake

This comes from an eighteenth-century cookbook, from a time when tomatoes were more plentiful than pineapples. Add more tomatoes from the garden if they are bursting with juicy flavor.

$^1/_2$ cup (1 stick) unsalted butter, melted
1 tablespoon grated fresh ginger
6 tablespoons light brown sugar
2 to 3 ripe tomatoes (or enough to cover the bottom
    of the pan as you would a pineapple upside-
    down cake), skinned, seeded and sliced
    $^1/_4$ inch thick
$^1/_2$ cup (1 stick) unsalted butter

1 $^1/_2$ cups brown sugar
$^1/_2$ cup molasses
2 $^1/_2$ cups unbleached white flour
2 teaspoons baking powder
1 tablespoon ground ginger
$^1/_2$ teaspoon ground cloves
1 cup buttermilk
Whipped cream (optional)

Preheat the oven to 350 degrees F.

Combine the melted butter with the ginger and light brown sugar and spread evenly on the bottom of a 10-by-14-inch baking pan. Cover with tomato slices.

Meanwhile, in a mixer, cream the butter with the brown sugar and molasses. In another bowl, sift together the flour, baking powder and spices. Add the flour mixture alternately with the buttermilk to the creamed butter and sugar and mix until fully incorporated. Pour the batter over the tomatoes in the baking pan.

Bake for approximately 40 minutes, or until a toothpick inserted into the center comes out clean. Remove from the oven. To unmold, loosen the outer edges with a dull knife, place a large platter over the baking pan and quickly invert the pan and the platter. Let stand at least 5 minutes before removing the pan. Serve warm with whipped cream, if desired. *Serves 6*

Pumpkin and Chutney Kolaches

This Czech version of a Danish pastry was discovered by Regina Schrambling while she was living in Nebraska. The not-too-sweet dough takes quite well to pumpkin. The filling is usually made from apricots or poppy seeds, but the chutney works better in this version. These are best eaten the same day they're baked.

1 package (scant 1 tablespoon) active dry yeast
4 to 4 1/2 cups all-purpose flour
1/2 cup (1 stick) unsalted butter, softened, plus
    2 tablespoons, melted
1/2 cup milk
3/4 cup granulated sugar

1/4 teaspoon salt
2 large egg yolks, at room temperature
1/2 cup cooked and puréed fresh pumpkin
    (or 1/2 cup canned)
1/2 cup mango chutney, finely chopped

In a large bowl, combine the yeast and 1 1/2 cups of the flour. In a small saucepan, combine the 1/2 cup butter, milk, sugar and salt and heat until just scalded (approximately 115 degrees F.). Pour the warm mixture into the yeast mixture. Add the egg yolks and pumpkin and, using an electric mixer set on low speed, beat for 1 minute. Increase the speed to high and beat for 3 minutes longer. Using a wooden spoon, stir in enough of the remaining 2 1/2 to 3 cups flour to make a soft dough.

Turn out the dough onto a lightly floured surface and knead for 8 to 10 minutes, or until soft and elastic. Shape into a ball and place in a well-buttered bowl. Turn the dough to coat the surface with butter. Cover the bowl with a kitchen towel and let the dough rise in a warm, draft-free spot for approximately 1 1/2 hours, or until doubled in bulk.

Punch down the dough. Tear off pieces approximately the size of golf balls and form into smooth balls. Lightly butter several baking sheets. Arrange 3 inches apart on the baking sheets. Cover with a kitchen towel and let the dough rise again for approximately 45 minutes, or until doubled in bulk.

Preheat the oven to 400 degrees F.

When the rolls have risen, flatten them slightly and make a small depression in the center of each. Spoon approximately 1 teaspoon of the chutney in each depression. Brush the rolls lightly with melted butter.

Bake 12 to 15 minutes, until golden brown. Serve warm. *Makes approximately 2 dozen kolaches*

Banana and Butternut Squash Bread with Mace and Pecans

*Double your nutrients and your flavors: This bread is a hybrid of classics
using banana and squash. Vary the spices and add different nuts if you wish.*

1 cup granulated sugar
$^1/_2$ cup (1 stick) unsalted butter, softened
$^3/_4$ cup mashed very ripe banana (1 to 2 bananas)
1 cup cooked and mashed butternut or other
    winter squash
2 large eggs
1 teaspoon vanilla extract
2 cups all-purpose flour

1 teaspoon baking soda
$^1/_2$ teaspoon baking powder
$^1/_2$ teaspoon salt
1 teaspoon ground mace
$^1/_2$ teaspoon freshly grated nutmeg
1 cup coarsely chopped pecans or walnuts
$^1/_2$ cup toasted, hulled pumpkin seeds (optional)

Preheat the oven to 350 degrees F. Butter a 9-by-5-inch loaf pan, preferably glass.

    In a large bowl and using an electric mixer set on medium speed, beat together the sugar and butter until light. Beat in the banana and squash. Add the eggs, beating until smooth, then mix in the vanilla.

    In another bowl, stir together the flour, baking soda, baking powder, salt, mace and nutmeg.

Add the flour mixture to the butter mixture, beating until smooth. Stir in the nuts. Spread the batter into the prepared pan and sprinkle with pumpkin seeds, if desired.

    Bake for 50 to 60 minutes, or until a toothpick inserted in the center comes out clean. Let cool completely on a rack before slicing. *Makes 1 loaf*

Tomato Spice Tea Bread

This recipe was shared by Beth Hensperger, author, teacher and bread-baking expert.
Once you gather the ingredients, the bread is prepared and baked within an hour.

2 large ripe tomatoes
2 eggs
¹/₃ cup vegetable oil
¹/₂ cup granulated sugar
¹/₂ cup light brown sugar

1 ¹/₂ cups unbleached white flour
1 teaspoon ground cinnamon
¹/₂ teaspoon baking powder
Pinch of salt
¹/₄ cup sliced almonds

Preheat the oven to 350 degrees F. Grease a 6-cup Bundt pan or an 8-inch loaf pan. Set aside.

Peel and seed the tomatoes. In a blender or food processor fitted with a metal blade, coarsely purée the tomatoes. Measure out 1 ¹/₄ cups purée.

With an electric mixer, blend the eggs, oil and sugars. Beat at high speed for approximately 3 minutes, or until the mixture is light and fluffy. Add the tomato purée and mix well.

In a large bowl, combine all the dry ingredients except the almonds, then gradually add the dry ingredients to the moist. Beat at medium speed until thoroughly blended. The batter will be thin.

Pour the batter evenly into the pan. Sprinkle the top with almonds. Bake for approximately 40 minutes, or until a toothpick inserted into the center comes out clean. Let cool in the pan for 5 minutes, turn out onto a rack and let cool completely before cutting into thin slices. *Makes 1 loaf*

Mango and Crystallized Ginger Quick Bread

The sunny flavors of the tropics are packed in this light quick bread,
perfect for a foggy morning or a hot afternoon.

¹/₂ cup (1 stick) butter
1 cup granulated sugar
3 eggs
1 cup fresh mango purée (2 to 3 mangoes,
*   depending on their size)*

2 cups all-purpose flour
1 teaspoon baking soda
¹/₄ teaspoon salt
¹/₂ cup (3 ounces) crystallized ginger, cut into
*   small dice*

Preheat the oven to 350 degrees F. Butter a 9-by-5-inch loaf pan.

In a large bowl with an electric mixer, beat the butter and sugar until well blended. Add the eggs, one at a time, and continue beating until the mixture is creamy. Stir in the mango purée. (The mixture will look "separated," but will come back together when the dry ingredients are added.)

In a small bowl, combine flour, baking soda and salt. Using a wooden spoon, stir the dry ingredients into the creamy mixture. Be careful not to overmix.

Using a rubber spatula, gently fold in the crystallized ginger.

Spoon the batter into the loaf pan. Bake for 1 hour. The cake should be golden brown and feel firm when lightly pressed with your fingertips. Let cool in the pan for 15 minutes, then transfer to a cooling rack. *Makes 1 loaf*

Savory Zucchini and Cheese Madeleines

A French madeleine mold converts a quichelike filling into a breakfast or teatime treat with a crunchy crust and moist center. If you don't have a madeleine mold, use miniature muffin tins and bake for 15 minutes.

2 large eggs
2 tablespoons heavy cream
2 teaspoons Creole or Pommery (coarse-grain)
    mustard
2 tablespoons (¹/4 stick) unsalted butter, melted
3 cloves garlic, minced
1 ¹/2 teaspoons dried basil, crumbled
1 teaspoon salt
¹/4 teaspoon freshly ground black pepper

Dash of cayenne pepper
1 cup all-purpose flour
¹/2 teaspoon baking powder
¹/4 cup coarse-grind yellow cornmeal
2 cups firmly packed, coarsely grated zucchini
    (approximately 3 squash)
1 small yellow onion, finely diced
1 small red bell pepper, cored, seeded and finely diced
1 cup grated Gruyère or Jarlsberg cheese

Preheat the oven to 425 degrees F. Oil 3 madeleine molds. (If you have only 1 mold, work in batches, letting the mold cool before refilling.)

In a large bowl, combine the eggs, cream, mustard, melted butter, garlic, basil, salt and black and cayenne peppers and mix well. Stir in the flour, baking powder and cornmeal and mix well. Add the zucchini, onion, bell pepper and cheese and mix thoroughly. Spoon into the madeleine molds.

Bake in the oven 20 minutes, or until puffed and golden brown (the centers will still be moist). Turn out of the molds and serve warm, or let cool on wire racks to room temperature. *Makes approximately 3 dozen madeleines*

Skillet Corn Bread

Although this corn bread can be baked in a pie pan, baking dish or cast-iron skillet (which creates the best crust), an iron mold for corn sticks adds character and dresses up an old standby, especially for parties. The sugar is optional—it is generally frowned upon by Southerners, and omitting it shows off the natural corn sweetness.

2 tablespoons vegetable oil or bacon grease
3/4 cup fine yellow cornmeal
1 cup all-purpose unbleached flour
4 tablespoons granulated sugar (optional)
2 teaspoons baking powder

1/2 teaspoon salt
1 egg
2 tablespoons (1/4 stick) unsalted butter, melted
1 cup buttermilk

Preheat the oven to 425 degrees F.

Pour the oil into several corn stick molds or a 9-inch cast-iron skillet and place it in the hot oven.

In a large mixing bowl, combine the cornmeal, flour, sugar, if desired, baking powder and salt. Make a well in the mixture and add the egg, butter and buttermilk. Using a wooden spoon or a whisk, gradually incorporate the wet ingredients into the dry, then continue to beat for 2 minutes.

To make corn sticks, pour the batter into the molds approximately two-thirds full and bake for 15 minutes, or until golden brown.

To make corn bread, pour the batter carefully into the heated skillet and bake for 20 minutes, or until an inserted knife comes out clean and the top is golden brown. *Serves 4 to 6*

Onion Confit Overnight Breakfast Rolls

I love this breakfast roll recipe because almost all the work takes place the night before. The dough rises in the refrigerator while you sleep, and in the morning the elements come together in no time at all, baking into light, tender rolls. If you have adventurous eaters who don't mind garlic for breakfast, cook a few cloves into the confit. Serve the rolls with sweet butter and cups of dark rich coffee.

4 tablespoons ($^1/_2$ stick) unsalted butter, melted
$^1/_2$ cup milk
1 tablespoon granulated sugar
1 egg, lightly beaten
2 $^1/_4$ cups unbleached white flour
1 package (scant 1 tablespoon) active dry yeast
$^3/_4$ teaspoon salt
$^1/_2$ teaspoon freshly ground black pepper

Confit:
1 tablespoon unsalted butter
1 tablespoon olive oil
2 pounds onions or shallots, thinly sliced
4 cloves garlic, thinly sliced (optional)
Pinch of salt

1 egg yolk
1 tablespoon water

To make the dough, in a small saucepan over low heat, combine the butter, milk and sugar and heat until the butter is melted. Cool to approximately 120 degrees F.

While the butter is melting, in a large mixing bowl or in the bowl of an electric mixer fitted with the paddle attachment, combine the egg, flour, yeast, salt and pepper. Gradually add the warm liquid to the dry ingredients while beating with a spoon or the paddle attachment. Continue to beat for approximately 3 minutes, or until the mixture forms a soft dough. Transfer to a clean bowl, cover and refrigerate overnight.

To make the confit, in a heavy-bottomed sauté pan over low heat, melt the butter with the oil. Add the onions and the garlic, if desired, and sauté until very soft, approximately 40 minutes to 1 hour. Season with salt, let cool, cover and refrigerate overnight.

In the morning, preheat the oven to 375 degrees F. Lightly oil a baking sheet.

Turn out the dough onto a lightly floured work surface and divide into 3 equal pieces. Roll each piece into a round approximately $^1/_8$ inch thick. Cover each round with one-third of the confit. Cut each round into 4 equal wedges.

To make the rolls, begin at the wide end of each wedge and roll up the wedge, ending with the point visible. Place the pointed side down on the baking sheet. Repeat until all of the rolls are formed, then let them sit for approximately 15 minutes.

In a small bowl, whisk together the egg yolk and water. Brush the tops of the rolls generously with the egg wash. Bake for approximately 12 minutes, or until golden brown. Serve warm. *Makes 12 rolls*

Tea Sandwiches

Tiny sandwiches are to a formal tea what muffins are to breakfast—quintessential. They are the visual high point, and when prepared correctly, their simplicity commands the respect of both the Queen and Emily Post.

After choosing a base—be it white, wheat, rye or pumpernickel breads, scones, biscuits or crackers—the choice of toppings is limited only by preference and available ingredients. Choose complementary spreads in which the flavor of one ingredient doesn't overpower the next.

A bit of butter or cream cheese on the bread will keep colorful, edible flowers such as pansies, nasturtiums, calendula and lilies in place. Smoked or fresh fish with spreads such as Goat Cheese with Mille Herbes or Parsley and Chive Butter works well. Cured or smoked meats are complemented by Cranberry Butter.

For children's and other special teas, I love to cut the bread with fanciful cookie cutters. Also consider apple slices, jícama and cucumber rounds as alternative canapé bases.

Lemon Cucumber Tea Sandwiches

*These are a tart, refreshing change
from the tried-and-true cucumber sandwiches
typically served with tea.*

*6 tablespoons (³/4 stick) unsalted butter,
    at room temperature
Grated zest of 1 lemon
1 tablespoon lemon juice with pulp
12 thin slices white or whole-wheat bread
1 small cucumber, peeled and thinly sliced
Granulated sugar, to taste
Freshly ground black pepper, to taste*

In a small bowl, cream the butter with the zest
and lemon juice.

Evenly spread a light film of butter on each
slice of bread. Cover half the bread slices with a
thin layer of cucumber.

Sprinkle lightly with sugar and pepper. Cover
with the remaining buttered bread slices, trim
the crusts and cut each sandwich into 4 triangles.
Makes 24 sandwiches

Lemon Sandwiches

*Serve these with an herbal lemon tea
or black tea. They are especially nice served
next to a shrimp or fish paté.*

*4 tablespoons (¹/2 stick) unsalted butter,
    at room temperature
6 thin slices dense three-grain wheat bread
1 lemon, thinly sliced and seeds removed
Salt and freshly ground black pepper, to taste*

Generously butter the bread. Cover half the bread
slices with the lemon slices and season with salt
and pepper. Cover with the remaining buttered
slices and cut each sandwich into 4 triangles.
Makes 24 sandwiches

Artist's Palette Herb Flower Canapés

Almost all the culinary herbs are suitable for these artistic one-of-a-kind treats, so harvest
a fanciful variety of sprigs and blossoms. If you lack an herb garden, purchase a bunch each
of Italian parsley, dill, thyme and basil. Edible flowers can be found at specialty produce markets.
(Avoid flowers from florist shops, as they are commonly sprayed with unsuitable chemicals.)
Use rustic, dense loaves for the canapé bases; softer breads will not hold up.

1/2 pound natural cream cheese, at room temperature
3 tablespoons finely chopped fresh chives
3 to 5 tablespoons milk
2 large rectangular loaves firm dense bread, unsliced

40 to 60 fresh herb flowers
20 to 30 fresh edible flowers
20 to 30 fresh herb sprigs

Place the cream cheese in a mixing bowl. Add the chives and 3 tablespoons of the milk and stir until smooth. If the mixture is too thick, add more milk as needed to thin to the correct consistency.

Using a serrated knife, trim the crusts from the loaves of bread. Cut the loaves into slices 1/3 inch thick. Cut each slice into 2 1/2- to 4-inch squares, 2-by-3-inch rectangles or 3-inch triangles. Spread the cream cheese mixture on the bread cutouts (use approximately 1 tablespoon per 2 1/2-inch square). Arrange the cutouts on baking sheets, cover with plastic wrap and refrigerate for up to 6 hours.

If possible, pick the herb flowers in the early morning, when they are at their freshest. Choose from the flowers of borage, both common and garlic chives, chamomile, chervil, cilantro, dill,

oregano, rosemary, sage, sweet marjoram and thyme. If you have edible flowers, pick them as well. Select nasturtiums, pansies, violets and/or violas. (Caution: Be sure the flowers you pick are indeed edible, and that they have not been sprayed with pesticides unsuitable for edible plants.) Gently rinse all the flowers and stand them in water in the refrigerator for up to 6 hours.

Use herb leaves to fill out the designs. Italian and curly-leaf parsleys, mint, dill, purple and sweet basils, sweet marjoram, oregano, thyme and variegated sages all work well. Carefully wash the leaves and gently pat them dry on paper towels. Lay them out on a baking sheet lined with damp paper towels and cover with plastic wrap. Refrigerate for up to 2 hours.

To assemble the canapés, decorate each cutout with an herb flower or an edible flower

or two. Add a few contrasting herb leaves. Use your imagination when mixing the different colors and textures. The hors d'oeuvre may be prepared a few hours in advance, covered with plastic wrap and refrigerated, but the less time before serving, the fresher the flowers will be. To unify the design, put a paper doily on a decorative tray and transfer the hors d'oeuvres to the tray. Serve at once. *Serves 8 to 10*

Open-Faced Watercress Sandwiches

*Dainty, crustless watercress sandwiches are
the epitome of refinement at formal teas.
Nasturtium flowers add their own mild spiciness
and make a jewel-like garnish.*

1 large bunch watercress
30 nasturtium flowers
$^1/_4$ cup very finely chopped yellow onion
$^1/_2$ cup peeled, seeded, and finely chopped cucumber
$^1/_2$ teaspoon salt
$^1/_8$ teaspoon freshly ground black pepper
$^1/_2$ pound natural cream cheese, softened
8 slices fine-grained, sweet country white,
        wheat, or egg bread

Wash and dry the watercress and discard the tough
stems. Set aside a handful of the watercress leaves
for garnish. Finely chop the rest, which should
yield a good $^1/_2$ cup. Wash and dry the nasturtium flowers, checking carefully for bugs that like
to hide inside. Set aside 8 flowers for garnish and
finely julienne the rest.

   In a medium bowl, mix the onion, cucumber, chopped watercress and flowers, salt and
pepper into the softened cream cheese. Let the
flavors blend for at least 1 hour.

   Spread the mixture on the bread slices and
garnish with the remaining watercress leaves and
a confetti of the whole nasturtium petals. These
sandwiches are lovely open-faced, but closed
they are a treat for the lunch box or for a picnic.
Serves 4

Additional Tea Sandwich Ideas

*Try these additional tea sandwich suggestions using
the toppings from the Spreads chapter.*

Smoked salmon with cream cheese and
        Goat Cheese with Mille Herbes
Thinly sliced turkey with cranberries and
        Cranberry Butter
Sun-dried tomato strips with Tomato Tapenade
Dollop of creamed tuna or turkey with
        Parsley and Chive Butter
Grilled rounds of Japanese eggplant with
        Goat Cheese with Mille Herbes
Slivers of roasted quail with
        Meyer Lemon Marmalade
Thinly sliced radishes with Herb Flower Butter or
        Parsley and Chive Butter
Tiny rounds of pork tenderloin with Apple Butter
Strips of deli ham with Mediterranean Herb Honey
        or Parsley and Chive Butter
Sautéed chorizo slices with
        Jalapeño and Cumin Butter

To make the best tea sandwiches, choose thin,
dense bread slices cut into triangles, squares and
circles or shaped with cookie cutters. Spread a
thin layer of butter or jam on the bread, then top
with the ingredients of your choice.

Spreads

From delicate bowls of glistening marmalades and tiny pots of flavored butters come the *pièces de résistance* for homemade muffins, scones, biscuits and breads. One bite of their tantalizing flavors, and scones or biscuits will be on the table as fast as you can combine the ingredients and bake them in the oven.

From the sweet selection, berry jams and marmalades of apricots, oranges and lemons are made in batches large enough to preserve in canning jars. Flavored honeys, which add herbal essences to the all-time classic biscuit spread, are best steeped for a week before use.

Butters flavored with herb flowers and spices, on the other hand, can be made shortly before use. After one taste of the Goat Cheese with Mille Herbes, you'll understand why it is a staple in my house. The same goes for Sweet and Spicy Red Onion Marmalade and Tomato Tapenade, two highlights on any tea or breakfast table.

Lemon Curd

*Serve Lemon Curd with scones, muffins,
toast or fresh berries, or use it as a tangy filling
in prebaked miniature tart shells.*

4 egg yolks, at room temperature
$1/2$ cup granulated sugar
Grated zest of 1 lemon
$1/2$ cup fresh lemon juice

In a small stainless steel bowl or in the top of a double boiler, whisk together the egg yolks and sugar. Add the zest and whisk in the lemon juice. Set over a pot of simmering water and whisk constantly until the mixture thickens, approximately 10 minutes.

Remove from the heat and strain the mixture through a fine sieve into a glass or ceramic container. Cover with plastic wrap and refrigerate until cool. *Makes approximately 1 cup*

Clotted Cream

*To make the real thing, you must start with a cow
and fresh, unpasteurized cream. For anyone who
has ever eaten clotted cream in Devonshire, there is
nothing else like it. However, so as not to deprive
ourselves, here is a variation of it for those without
cows. The unsweetened cream is lovely with ripe
berries and is a classic on scones with preserves.*

1 cup heavy (whipping) or Devon cream
1 teaspoon lemon juice

In the bowl of an electric mixer, beat the cream and lemon juice on medium speed until beginning to thicken, approximately 3 to 4 minutes. Do not scrape down the sides while it is mixing. Then, turn up the speed to high and beat another few minutes. You should get a curd-like cream on the top and thick cream on the bottom. Mix the cream gently together. The consistency should resemble pudding before it is set. Serve cold. *Makes 1 $1/2$ cups*

Basic Master Strawberry Jam

This recipe uses a short-boil method with liquid pectin because it offers greater ease of preparation than powdered pectin. Liquid pectin requires little stirring while the jam is boiling.

7 half-pint jars and matching lids (use new lids only)
4 cups crushed strawberries (approximately 6 cups whole strawberries)

7 cups granulated sugar
One 3-ounce pouch liquid pectin (available in grocery stores)
1/2 teaspoon margarine

Sterilize the jars by washing and rinsing them in the dishwasher without detergent and keep warm under cloth towels. Put lids in a small pan, cover with water and boil for 10 minutes. Turn off heat, but keep the lids warm.

Rinse strawberries lightly, but do not bruise. Drain. Completely cut away the green caps and any damaged portions of fruit. Place the strawberries, a small amount at a time, in a food processor and pulse briefly, making sure to crush but not purée the berries. Repeat until all the strawberries are crushed.

Measure 4 cups of crushed strawberries. Place strawberries and sugar in a large kettle and mix thoroughly.

Open the liquid pectin pouch with scissors. Stand it upright in a cup while waiting for berries to boil. Bring strawberry mixture to a full, rolling boil over high heat. Add the margarine and continue to stir as it melts. Pour in the pectin all at once, stirring vigorously. When the mixture reaches a full, rolling boil again, stir for 1 minute.

Remove the kettle from the heat. Set in the sink and, using a metal spoon, skim off any foam. Transfer back to the stove or counter.

With a 1-cup measuring cup or ladle, fill jars with jam up to 1/8 inch from the rim. With a damp cloth, wipe the jar rims. (The rims of jars must be impeccably clean or they will not seal properly.) Quickly place lids on top and screw on tightly. Set the jars upside down on a dry towel. Cover and let stand for 5 minutes. Return to upright position. Cover with a large cloth towel and set aside to cool for 8 to 15 hours. Store in a cool, dark place for up to a year. Keep in the refrigerator once opened. *Makes 7 half-pints*

Red Raspberry Jam

Follow the Basic Master Strawberry Jam recipe except: Use 6 ½ cups of granulated sugar to 4 cups of crushed red raspberries. *Makes 7 half-pints*

Olallieberry Jam

Follow the Basic Master Strawberry Jam recipe except: Use 7 ½ cups of granulated sugar to 4 cups of crushed olallieberries. *Makes 7 ½ half-pints*

Raspberry and Cherry Preserves

The raspberries retain their seedy crunch and tartness,
while the cherries impart body and keep their shape.

2 pounds Bing cherries
8 cups raspberries
3 1/2 cups granulated sugar

2 tablespoons fresh lemon juice
4 half-pint jars and matching lids (use new lids only)

Stem and pit the cherries; you should have 4 cups. In a large bowl, stir together the cherries, raspberries and sugar. Let stand at room temperature, stirring occasionally, for 2 hours.

Pour the fruit into a wide, shallow nonreactive saucepan and stir in the lemon juice. Cook over moderate heat, stirring occasionally, for 30 to 40 minutes until the mixture looks thickened and glazed. Remove a tablespoon of the preserves to a small saucer and chill in the freezer for 5 minutes. Run your finger through the chilled mixture; if it wrinkles, it is ready to jar. If it is not ready, continue cooking for 5 more minutes and repeat the test.

Sterilize the jars by washing and rinsing them in the dishwasher without detergent; keep them warm in a 250-degree-F. oven. Pour boiling water over the jar lids to soften the rubber seals.

Ladle the hot preserves to within 1/2 inch of the rims of the jars. Wipe the rims and seal with the hot lids and metal bands. Let cool to room temperature, then refrigerate for several weeks. Or, to store longer, process in a water bath. Place the jars on a rack, without touching, in a large, deep pot with water to cover by one inch. Cover and boil for 15 minutes. Use tongs to remove the jars to a cooling rack and allow to cool to room temperature. Check the seals. The jars are sealed when the center of the lid is slightly indented and cannot be pressed in with a fingertip. *Makes 4 half-pints*

Cranberry and Nectarine Jam

*This is an example of a cross-season jam: Cranberries and nectarines are not
in the market at the same time. If you forgot to toss a couple of bags of cranberries into
the freezer last fall, most stores now stock them frozen year-round. Frozen cranberries
add natural pectin, tartness and vibrant color to the nectarines.*

5 large nectarines (approximately 1 pound)
2 cups granulated sugar
3 cups fresh or frozen cranberries (approximately
   3/4 pound)

1 tablespoon fresh lemon juice
4 half-pint jars and matching lids (use new
   lids only)

Cut the unpeeled nectarines into 1-inch chunks. Toss them in a large bowl with 1 cup of sugar. Set aside for 2 hours at room temperature.

In a large saucepan, stir together the cranberries and remaining 1 cup of sugar. Place over moderate heat and cook, stirring constantly, approximately 10 minutes, or until the cranberries pop. Stir in the nectarines and all of their juice. Add the lemon juice. Continue cooking over moderate heat, stirring occasionally, for 20 minutes, or until the mixture thickens.

Sterilize the jars by washing and rinsing them in the dishwasher without detergent; keep them warm in a 250-degree-F. oven. Pour boiling water over the jar lids to soften the rubber seals.

Ladle the hot jam into the jars, filling to within 1/2 inch of the top. Wipe the rims carefully and seal with the hot lids and metal bands. Place the jars on a rack, without touching, in a large, deep pot with water to cover by one inch. Cover and boil for 15 minutes. Use tongs to remove the jars to a cooling rack and allow to cool to room temperature. Check the seals. The jars are sealed when the center of the lid is slightly indented and cannot be pressed in with a fingertip. *Makes 4 half-pints*

Meyer Lemon Marmalade

Meyer lemons have more perfume and are sweeter and more flavorful than the usual lemon variety found in the grocery stores. Buy them when you see them. For lemon lovers, this marmalade rivals any orange marmalade from Seville. The Scotch is sure to be a topic of conversation at tea time.

1 pound Meyer or Eureka lemons
1 pound small sugar cubes

1 ounce single-malt Scotch whisky
3 half-pint jars and matching lids (use new lids only)

Wash and scrub the lemons. Place them in a large pot and cover with cold water. Bring to a boil, reduce the heat, and simmer for 30 minutes, or until the flesh can be easily pierced with a knife. Drain and set aside to cool.

Cut the lemons crosswise into very thin slices. In a nonreactive heavy pot, combine the lemon slices and sugar and place over low heat. Cook, stirring, until the sugar cubes dissolve. Bring to a boil, stirring often so that the lemons do not scorch on the bottom of the pot. Cook until the syrup reaches 200 degrees F. and the lemons are translucent. Skim off any foam, add the Scotch and continue cooking for approximately 5 minutes, or until the marmalade coats the back of a spoon.

Sterilize the jars by washing and rinsing them in the dishwasher without detergent; keep them warm in a 250-degree-F. oven. Pour boiling water over the lids to soften the rubber seals.

Ladle the hot marmalade into the hot jars, filling to within ¹/₂ inch of the top. Wipe the rims and seal with the hot lids and metal bands. Place the jars on a rack, without touching, in a large, deep pot with water to cover by 1 inch. Cover and boil for 15 minutes. Use tongs to remove the jars to a cooling rack and allow to cool to room temperature. Check the seals. The jars are sealed when the center of the lid is slightly indented and cannot be pressed in with a fingertip. *Makes 3 half-pints*

Apricot and Orange Marmalade

Two golden fruits combine successfully in this thick, sweet-tart marmalade.
Every bite has a chunk of apricot or orange in this glistening variation of a classic.

3 pounds apricots
2 tablespoons finely chopped orange zest
1 cup orange sections

²/₃ cup fresh orange juice
2 cups granulated sugar
3 half-pint jars and matching lids (use new lids only)

Pit and quarter the apricots. There should be approximately 9 cups. In a 12-inch skillet or sauté pan, combine the apricots, zest, orange sections, juice and sugar. Allow to stand for 1 hour at room temperature.

Cook the mixture over moderate heat, stirring occasionally, for 1 1/2 hours, or until mixture looks glazed and clear liquid is no longer visible. Continue cooking, stirring constantly, for another 30 minutes until the marmalade is thick.

Sterilize the jars by washing and rinsing them in the dishwasher without detergent; keep them warm in a 250-degree-F. oven. Pour boiling water over the lids to soften the rubber seals.

Ladle the hot marmalade into the hot jars, filling to within 1/2 inch of the top. Wipe the rims and seal with the hot lids and metal bands. Place the jars on a rack, without touching, in a large, deep pot with water to cover by 1 inch. Cover and boil for 15 minutes. Use tongs to remove the jars to a cooling rack and allow to cool to room temperature. Check the seals. The jars are sealed when the center of the lid is slightly indented and cannot be pressed in with a fingertip. *Makes 3 half-pints*

Honey Pear Jam

If you're in the habit of beginning your day with toasted bread, scones, biscuits or muffins and fruit preserves, you may want to double this luscious recipe.

2 large firm-but-ripe pears (preferably Forelle, Bartlett or Comice), halved, cored and cut into $^1/_4$-inch cubes
$^1/_2$ cup water
$^1/_4$ cup fresh lemon juice
$^1/_4$ cup pear eau-de-vie

$^1/_4$ teaspoon ground cinnamon
$^1/_4$ teaspoon ground cloves
$^1/_4$ teaspoon ground nutmeg
$^1/_2$ cup honey
Pinch of salt

In a heavy-bottomed saucepan, combine the pears, water, lemon juice, eau-de-vie and spices; mix well. Bring to a boil over high heat and cook 5 minutes, stirring frequently. Reduce the heat to medium and simmer 25 minutes, stirring occasionally, until almost all the liquid has evaporated and the pears are very tender.

Add the honey and salt and mix well. Cook 15 to 20 minutes, stirring frequently, until the mixture is thick and aromatic and the pears have broken down. Remove from the heat and let cool to room temperature. Transfer to a nonreactive container with a tight-fitting lid and store in the refrigerator for up to 2 months. *Makes approximately 1 cup*

Apple Butter

Truly Colonial America's first butter, it's best served to grown-ups
on toast and to kids on sandwiches. Depending on the sweetness of the fruit, it
can be made without the addition of sugar or spices for a true fruity flavor.

4 pounds tart apples (such as McIntosh), quartered,
*   with skins, pits and stems*
2 cups apple cider
4 to 5 cups granulated sugar

3 teaspoons ground cinnamon
2 teaspoons ground cloves
1 teaspoon ground allspice
4 half-pint jars and matching lids (use new lids only)

Combine the apples with the cider in a large heavy-bottomed saucepan and bring to a simmer over medium heat. Simmer for 25 minutes, or until the apples are soft, stirring from time to time to prevent the apples from sticking to the bottom of the pan.

Pass the apples through a food mill placed over a large bowl. Mix in the sugar and spices and place over low heat for 4 hours, stirring often so that the mixture does not scorch. When the mixture is thick, or when it sticks to a spoon and no rim of liquid separates around the edge, the butter is done.

Sterilize the jars by washing and rinsing them in the dishwasher without detergent; keep them warm in a 250-degree-F. oven. Pour boiling water over the jar lids to soften the rubber seals.

Ladle the hot apple butter into the hot jars, filling to within 1/4 inch of the rims. Wipe the rims and seal with the hot lids and metal bands. Let cool to room temperature, then refrigerate for up to 3 weeks. For longer storage, process in a water bath. Place the jars on a rack, without touching, in a large, deep pot with water to cover by one inch. Cover and boil for 15 minutes. Use tongs to remove the jars to a cooling rack and allow to cool to room temperature. Check the seals. The jars are sealed when the center of the lid is slightly indented and cannot be pressed in with a fingertip. *Makes approximately 4 half-pints*

Cranberry Butter

The sweet-tart combination of this butter is perfect on Buttermilk
Breakfast Scones with Dried Cranberries and Carrot Muffins with Raisins
and Dried Pineapple, as well as on waffles and pancakes.

2 cups (4 sticks) unsalted butter, at room temperature
1/2 cup cranberries, coarsely chopped (if frozen, chop
*   them frozen and let thaw)*
1/4 cup light brown sugar
1/4 cup honey
4 tablespoons ground walnuts
1/2 cup cranberry sauce★
1 tablespoon grated orange zest
1 teaspoon grated lemon zest
2 tablespoons buttermilk

In a large bowl, whip the softened butter at high speed with an electric mixer until it turns pale yellow, scraping the sides of the bowl to make sure all the butter gets whipped.

Add the cranberries, sugar, honey, walnuts, cranberry sauce and orange and lemon zests.

Whip at medium speed until the mixture turns light pink.

Add the buttermilk and whip until fully incorporated. The butter can be covered and stored in the mixing bowl or, using a rubber spatula, transferred to smaller bowls for storage. It can also be refrigerated for 5 minutes to firm up slightly and then shaped into a log approximately 1 inch in diameter for easy slicing into discs. Store well wrapped in the refrigerator for 1 to 2 weeks or freeze for up to 3 months. *Makes approximately 2 cups*

★Note: If using commercial whole cranberry sauce, empty the can into a small bowl, stir to loosen the sauce, then measure.

Herb Flower Butter

These herb flowers mimic the flavor of their leaves, but the taste is much milder. The colorful flecks add a mosaic touch to the butter, which makes a lovely spread for canapés and tea sandwiches.

1 cup mixed fresh dill, rosemary, chive and basil
   flowers and purple basil leaves

1 cup (2 sticks) unsalted butter, at room temperature
2 teaspoons lemon juice

Wash the flowers and basil leaves and dry gently with paper towels. Pull the petals off of the chive blossoms. With a sharp chef's knife, finely mince all the herb flowers, including petals, and the basil leaves. Place in a small bowl, add the butter and lemon juice and, using a wooden spoon, cream together until well blended.

The butter can be covered and stored in the mixing bowl or, using a rubber spatula, transferred to smaller bowls for storage. It can also be refrigerated for 5 minutes to firm up slightly and then shaped into a log approximately 1 inch in diameter for easy slicing into discs. Store well wrapped in the refrigerator for 1 to 2 weeks or freeze for up to 3 months. *Makes 1 cup*

Jalapeño and Cumin Butter

The flavors of the Southwest in this eye-opening butter will stimulate any appetite. It is especially good with Spicy Green Onion Corn Muffins.

2 teaspoons cumin seeds
1/2 cup (1 stick) unsalted butter, at room temperature

2 teaspoons finely chopped fresh or pickled jalapeños
2 tablespoons chopped fresh cilantro

In a dry skillet over medium heat, toast the cumin seeds until lightly brown and aromatic. Grind in an electric spice mill or with a mortar and pestle.

   In a small bowl, combine the cumin, butter, jalapeños and cilantro. Using a wooden spoon, cream together until well blended. Let sit an hour for flavors to marry. The butter can be covered and stored in the mixing bowl or, using a rubber spatula, transferred to smaller bowls for storage. It can also be refrigerated for 5 minutes to firm up slightly and then shaped into a log approximately 1 inch in diameter for easy slicing into discs. Store well wrapped in the refrigerator for 1 to 2 weeks or freeze for up to 3 months. *Makes 1/2 cup*

Parsley and Chive Butter

Although this recipe features parsley and chives, other fresh herbs—sweet basil, cilantro, dill, sweet marjoram, spearmint, rosemary, tarragon, thyme—would also be delicious whipped into softened butter. Such butters are wonderful spread on breakfast toast, biscuits or tea sandwiches.

2 tablespoons finely minced fresh Italian parsley
2 tablespoons finely minced fresh chives
1 cup (2 sticks) unsalted butter, at room temperature

2 teaspoons freshly squeezed lemon juice
2 teaspoons Dijon mustard
Salt, to taste

In a small bowl, combine the parsley, chives and butter. Using a wooden spoon, cream together until well blended. Add the lemon juice, mustard and salt and stir until thoroughly incorporated.

The butter can be covered and stored in the mixing bowl or, using a rubber spatula, transferred to smaller bowls for storage. It can also be refrigerated for 5 minutes to firm up slightly and then shaped into a log approximately 1 inch in diameter for easy slicing into discs. Store well wrapped in the refrigerator for 1 to 2 weeks or freeze for up to 3 months. *Makes 1 cup*

Mediterranean Herb Honey

*This honey is excellent drizzled over strawberries
or cherries or served with scones and biscuits.*

One 12-ounce jar clover or alfalfa honey
4 teaspoons herbes de Provence, crumbled

Remove the cap and foil covering from the honey
jar. Place the uncapped jar in a saucepan with 2
inches of water. Bring the water to a simmer and
warm the honey for 5 minutes.

Remove the jar from the water and immediately add the herbs. Cover tightly, then shake
the jar to distribute the herbs evenly. Place the jar
in a sunny window or a warm spot for up to 1
week to allow the flavors to blend.

When the flavor suits you, warm the honey
as before to liquefy, then strain. Discard the herbs
and immediately return the strained honey to the
jar. Cover tightly and store at room temperature
on a dark shelf for up to 6 months. If crystals
form, simply warm the honey again, as directed,
before using. *Makes 1 1/2 cups*

Garden Sage Honey

*Try this spread on the Parmesan Black Pepper
Pillows, or substitute dried lavender for the sage,
and use it in the recipe for Lavender Honey
and Sweet Fennel Biscuits.*

One 12-ounce jar clover or alfalfa honey
4 teaspoons dried sage leaves, crumbled

Remove the cap and foil covering from the honey
jar. Place the uncapped jar in a saucepan with 2
inches of water. Bring the water to a simmer and
warm the honey for 5 minutes.

Remove the jar from the water and immediately add the sage. Cover tightly, then shake
the jar to distribute the sage evenly. Place the jar
in a sunny window or a warm spot for up to 1
week to allow the flavors to blend.

When the flavor suits you, warm the honey
as before to liquefy, then strain. Discard the sage
and immediately return the strained honey to the
jar. Cover tightly and store at room temperature
on a dark shelf for up to 6 months. If crystals
form, simply warm the honey again, as directed,
before using. *Makes 1 1/2 cups*

Note: Use only dried herbs to infuse honey; fresh herbs can raise the moisture content of the honey,
causing molds and spoilage.

Tomato Tapenade

*The traditional potent Mediterranean olive spread develops an even richer dimension
with the addition of sun-dried tomatoes. A definite match for Sun-Dried Tomato Biscuits,
this tapenade is delicious on the pumpkin kolaches, too.*

¹/₄ cup dry-packed sun-dried tomatoes
¹/₄ cup pitted Kalamata olives
¹/₄ cup firmly packed fresh basil or parsley leaves
¹/₂ teaspoon Worcestershire sauce
1 teaspoon anchovy paste

2 tablespoons extra virgin olive oil
1 clove garlic, minced
Salt and freshly ground black pepper, to taste
Chopped fresh basil or parsley, for garnish

Place the sun-dried tomatoes in a small bowl
and cover with boiling water. Let stand approximately 15 minutes, or until soft. Drain well and
transfer to a blender or to a food processor fitted
with the metal blade. Add the olives, basil leaves,
Worcestershire sauce, anchovy paste and oil.

Purée to form a fairly smooth paste, scraping
down the sides of the container frequently. Stir
in the garlic and season with salt and pepper.
Transfer to a small bowl for serving and garnish
with the fresh basil or parsley. *Makes approximately
³/₄ cup*

Goat Cheese with Mille Herbes

The "thousand herbs" show off their combined flavors in this tangy cheese dip.
Spread it on savory scones or bite-size crackers, or use as a base for tea sandwiches.

10 1/2 ounces fresh goat cheese, at room temperature
2 teaspoons finely minced fresh tarragon
2 teaspoons finely minced fresh Italian parsley
2 teaspoons finely minced fresh sweet marjoram
2 teaspoons finely minced fresh thyme

2 teaspoons finely minced fresh dill
2 teaspoons finely minced fresh sweet basil
1 teaspoon finely minced fresh chives
Pinch of cayenne pepper
Low-fat milk, for thinning

In a medium bowl, combine the cheese, herbs and cayenne pepper. Stir until well blended. Add milk to thin to the desired consistency.

Cover the bowl with plastic wrap and refrigerate for 1 hour to blend the flavors. Bring to room temperature before serving. *Makes approximately 1 1/4 cups*

Sweet and Spicy Red Onion Marmalade

This is a recipe with endless possibilities. Serve the marmalade paired with cream cheese on top
of a toasted onion bagel, spread on Sun-Dried Tomato Biscuits or scoop into hot tortillas.

1 tablespoon olive oil
3 red onions, finely chopped
2 or 3 fresh jalapeño or other hot chili peppers,
    seeded and minced
$^1/_4$ cup dry-packed sun-dried tomatoes, minced
1 tart cooking apple, such as Granny Smith or
    pippin, quartered, cored, peeled and grated

$^1/_2$ cup golden raisins, chopped
$^3/_4$ cup red wine vinegar
1 cup firmly packed brown sugar
1 cinnamon stick
1 cup apple juice or water
Salt, to taste

In a large, heavy-bottomed saucepan over medium-low heat, warm the oil. Add the onions and chilies and sauté for approximately 45 minutes, or until the onions are soft.

Add all the remaining ingredients except the salt. Place over low heat and bring to a gentle simmer. Cook, uncovered, for approximately 1 hour, or until all the ingredients are soft and the marmalade begins to thicken. Stir frequently. If all the moisture has evaporated, but the onions aren't fully cooked, add more water and continue to cook until the mixture is reduced to a thick, jamlike consistency.

Remove from the heat. Season with salt. You may choose to add more chili pepper at this time. Store in the refrigerator for up to 2 weeks.
Makes approximately 2 pints

METRIC CONVERSIONS

Liquid Weights

U.S. Measurements	Metric Equivalents
1/4 teaspoon	1.23 ml
1/2 teaspoon	2.5 ml
3/4 teaspoon	3.7 ml
1 teaspoon	5 ml
1 dessertspoon	10 ml
1 tablespoon (3 teaspoons)	15 ml
2 tablespoons (1 ounce)	30 ml
1/4 cup	60 ml
1/3 cup	80 ml
1/2 cup	120 ml
2/3 cup	160 ml
3/4 cup	180 ml
1 cup (8 ounces)	240 ml
2 cups (1 pint)	480 ml
3 cups	720 ml
4 cups (1 quart)	1 liter
4 quarts (1 gallon)	3 3/4 liters

Dry Weights

U.S. Measurements	Metric Equivalents
1/4 ounce	7 grams
1/3 ounce	10 grams
1/2 ounce	14 grams
1 ounce	28 grams
1 1/2 ounces	42 grams
1 3/4 ounces	50 grams
2 ounces	57 grams
3 1/2 ounces	100 grams
4 ounces (1/4 pound)	114 grams
6 ounces	170 grams
8 ounces (1/2 pound)	227 grams
9 ounces	250 grams
16 ounces (1 pound)	464 grams

Temperatures

Fahrenheit	Celsius (Centigrade)
32°F (water freezes)	0°C
200°F	95°C
212°F (water boils)	100°C
250°F	120°C
275°F	135°C
300°F (slow oven)	150°C
325°F	160°C
350°F (moderate oven)	175°C
375°F	190°C
400°F (hot oven)	205°C
425°F	220°C
450°F (very hot oven)	230°C
475°F	245°C
500°F (extremely hot oven)	260°C

Length

U.S. Measurements	Metric Equivalents
1/8 inch	3 mm
1/4 inch	6 mm
3/8 inch	1 cm
1/2 inch	1.2 cm
3/4 inch	2 cm
1 inch	2.5 cm
1 1/4 inches	3.1 cm
1 1/2 inches	3.7 cm
2 inches	5 cm
3 inches	7.5 cm
4 inches	10 cm

Approximate Equivalents

1 kilo is slightly more than 2 pounds
1 liter is slightly more than 1 quart
1 centimeter is approximately 3/8 inch

INDEX